THE FULL MONTY

Book by
Terrence McNally

Music and Lyrics by
David Yazbek

The original Broadway cast recording is available on RCA Victor

In Australia Contact:

Hal Leonard Australia Pty. Ltd.
22 Taunton Drive P.O. Box 5130
Cheltenham East, 3192 Victoria, Australia
Email: ausadmin@halleonard.com

ISBN 0-634-05380-9

7777 W. BLUEMOUND RD. P.O. BOX 13819 MILWAUKEE, WI 53213

Visit Hal Leonard Online at
www.halleonard.com

Photo by Carol Rosegg

DAVID YAZBEK is a recording artist, composer/lyricist, record producer and screenwriter whose album *The Laughing Man* won the 1997 AFIM Award for Best Pop Album of the Year. His other albums include *Tock* (1999) and *Damascus* (2001). He also won an Emmy Award for comedy writing a while back. *The Full Monty* is his first Broadway musical. More can be learned at www.davidyazbek.com.

10 It's a Woman's World

18 Man

32 Big-Ass Rock

25 Life With Harold

40 Big Black Man

47 You Rule My World

54 Jeanette's Showbiz Number

62 Breeze Off the River

72 You Walk With Me

67 You Rule My World (Reprise)

76 Let It Go

THE FULL MONTY

IT'S A WOMAN'S WORLD

Words and Music by
DAVID YAZBEK

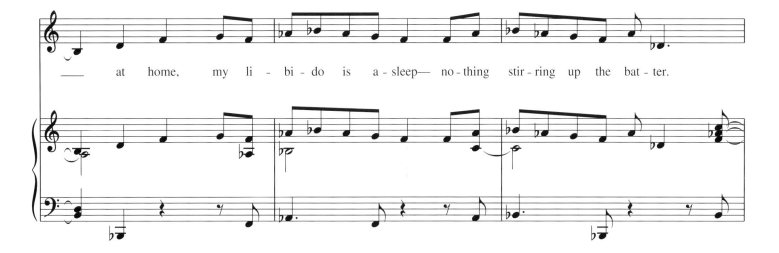

at home, my li - bi - do is a - sleep— no - thing stir - ring up the bat - ter.

Now I know all I need - ed was a heap o' danc - ing

beef - cake on a plat - ter. A sil - ver plat - ter! Let's ___ get sweat - y and let's _

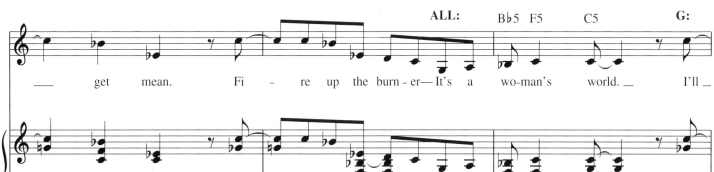

__ get mean. Fi - re up the burn - er—It's a wo - man's world. ___ I'll _

G. I. Joe ___ with the mil - i - ta - ry jock, I'd give a hund-red bucks to see what's in - side

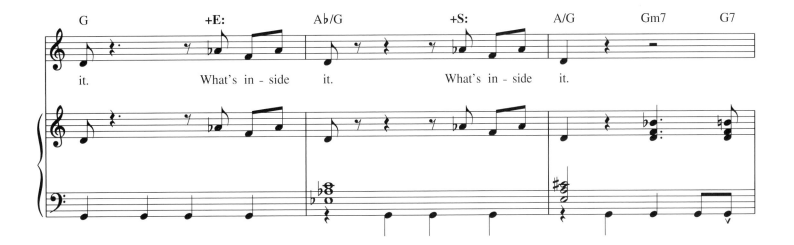

it. What's in - side it. What's in - side it.

Why do they hide it? All ___ that mu - sic and all ___ that beat, ma -

All ___ that mu - sic all ___ that beat, ma -

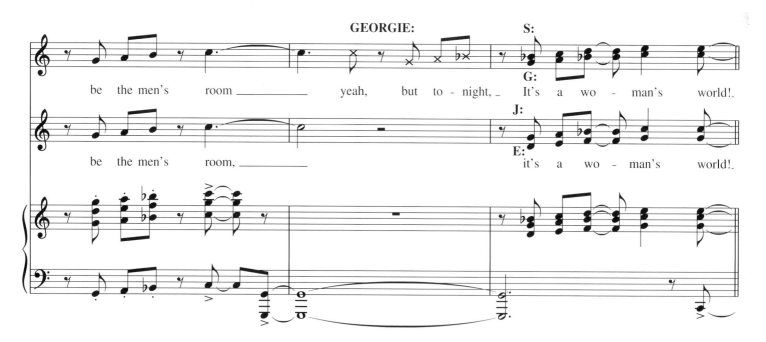

It's a wo-man's world! _

It's a wo-man's world! _

It's a wo-man's world! _____

It's a wo-man's world! _____

MAN

Words and Music by
DAVID YAZBEK

Steady

JERRY:

You're out of work. Your pride is miss-in'. They call you jerk but you don't lis-ten. You have-n't got a pot to piss in but you're a...

8vb throughout

loco

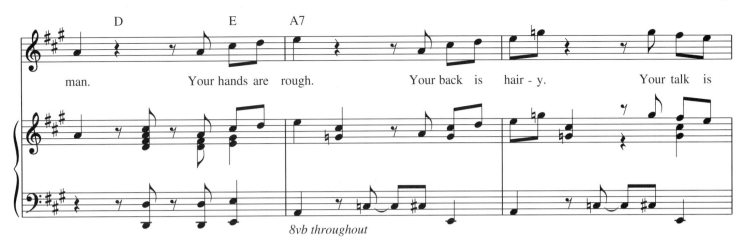

D   E   A7

man.   Your hands are rough.   Your back is hair-y.   Your talk is

8vb throughout

D7   A7

tough.   Your smell is scar-y.   Here's what you're not—   you're not a

E   F   E   D   E

fair-y.   No you're a beer drink-in' real live __ man.

loco

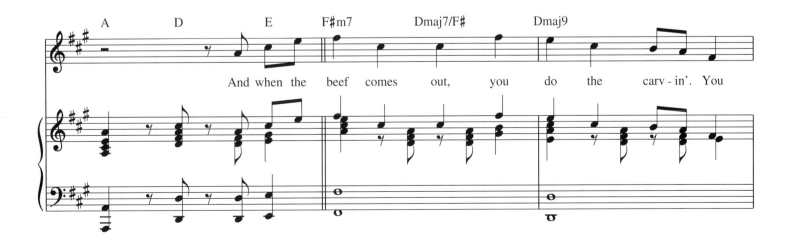

A   D   E   F#m7   Dmaj7/F#   Dmaj9

And when the beef comes out,   you do the carv-in'. You

plans. They al-ways fail. __ You've been di-vorced. You've been to

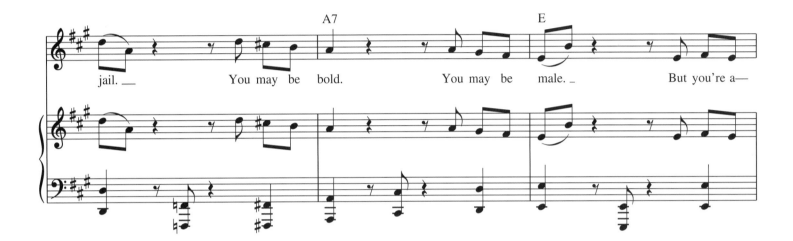

jail. __ You may be bold. You may be male. _ But you're a—

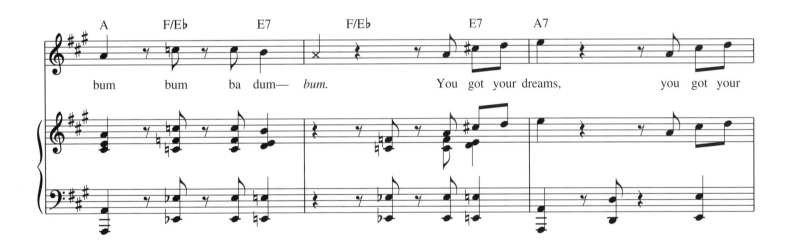

bum bum ba dum— *bum.* You got your dreams, you got your

wish-es and I don't want to sound ma-li-cious but you're a

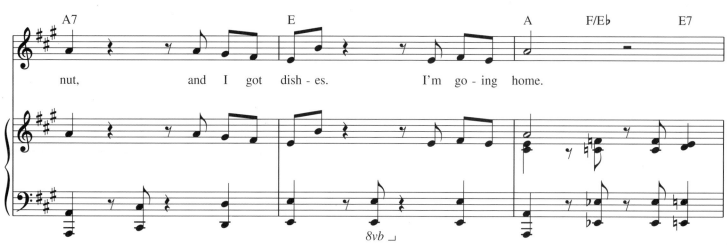

nut,   and I got dish - es.   I'm go - ing home.

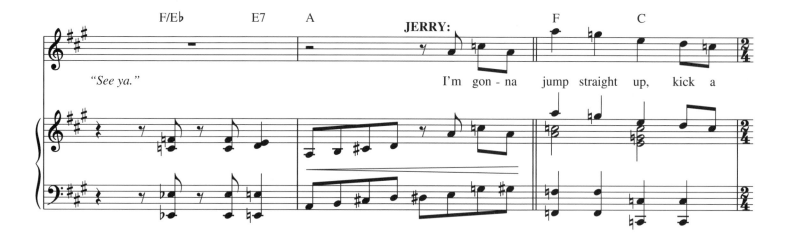

JERRY:

"See ya."   I'm gon - na jump straight up, kick a

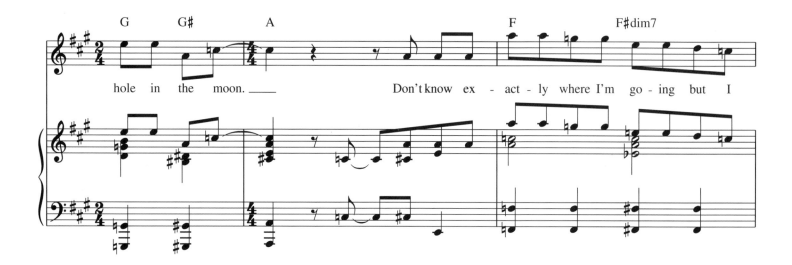

hole in the moon. ____ Don't know ex - act - ly where I'm go - ing but I

know I'm gon - na get there soon. ___ I'll show you.   I'll show them all. ___

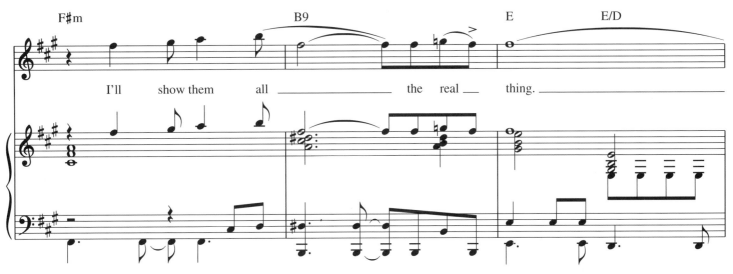

I'll show them all _____ the real ___ thing. _____

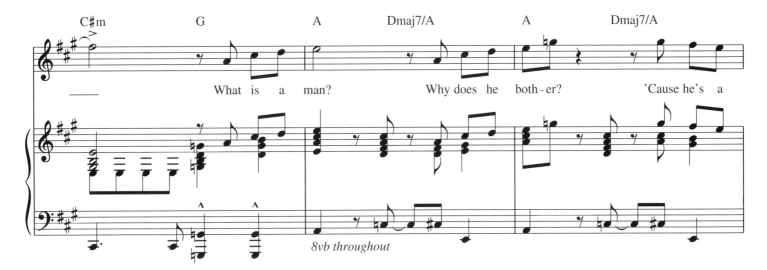

___ What is a man? Why does he both-er? 'Cause he's a

8vb throughout

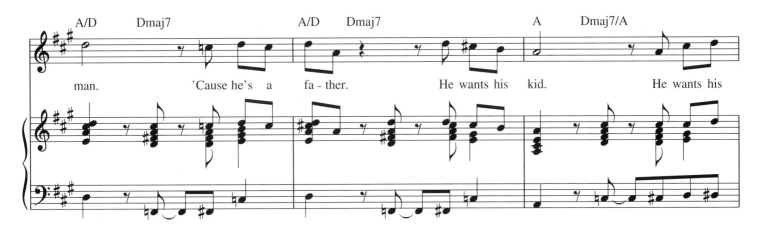

man. 'Cause he's a fa-ther. He wants his kid. He wants his

life. He wants to— da da da na na da na na— He wants to

loco

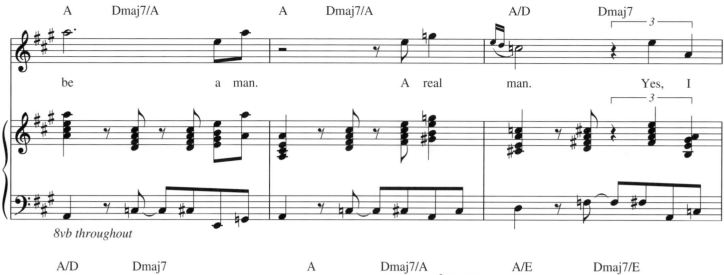

8vb throughout

be   a man.   A real   man.   Yes,   I

am. ___   I'm gon - na   be,   I've got - ta   be   a real ___

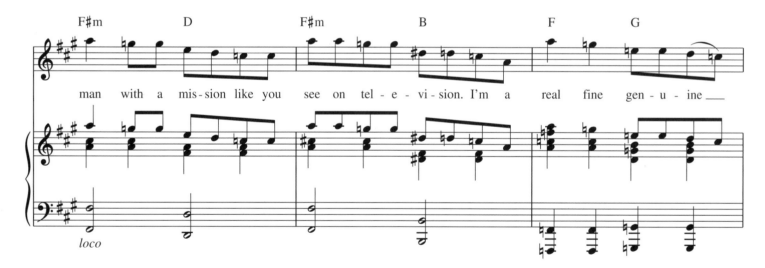

loco

man   with a mis - sion like you   see on tel - e - vi - sion. I'm a   real   fine   gen - u - ine ___

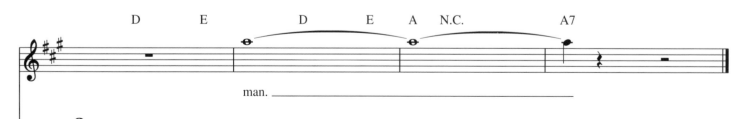

man. _____

LIFE WITH HAROLD

Words and Music by
DAVID YAZBEK

Mambo

VICKI:

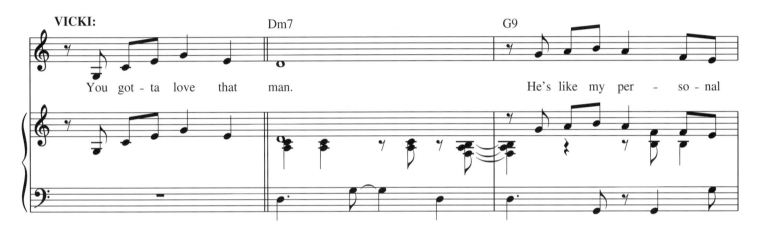

You got-ta love that man. He's like my per - so - nal

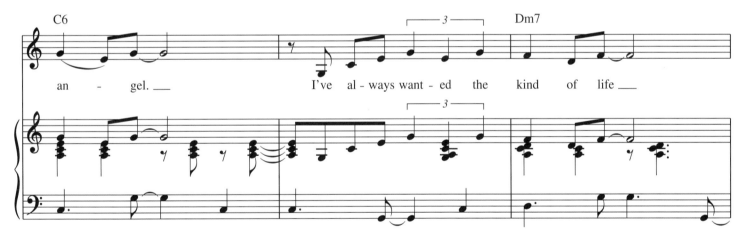

an - gel. ___ I've al-ways want-ed the kind of life ___

that I've been hav-ing as Har - old's ___ wife. What a

catch I have caught. He would buy me the moon if the

moon could be bought. I'm tell-in' you: ___ You got-ta love that

man. I real-ly love ___

___ that man. He likes me dressed to the nines.

I say two words and then "Ta - da!" __ There's me com-plete - ly in

Pra - da. __ And I've got the boots that go with the

belt that goes with the bag that goes with my won - der - ful life with

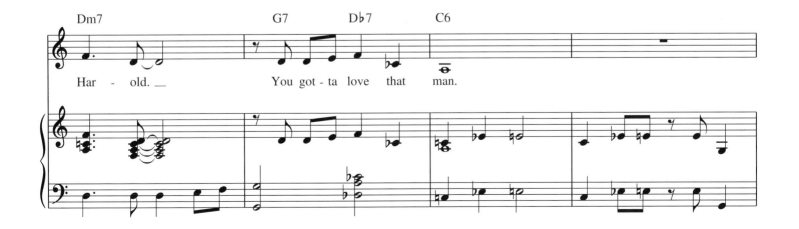

Har - old. __ You got - ta love that man.

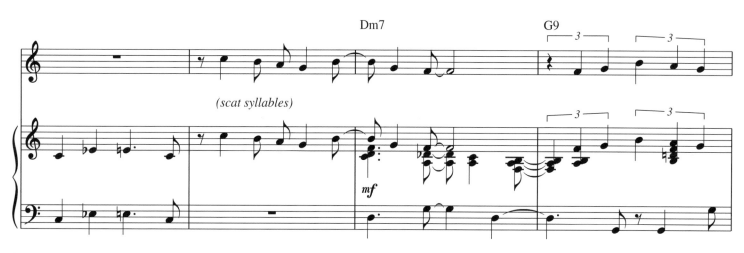

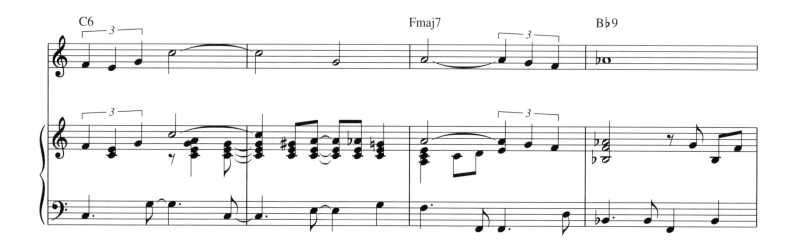

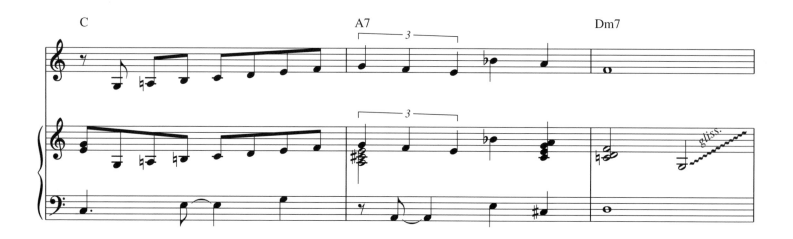

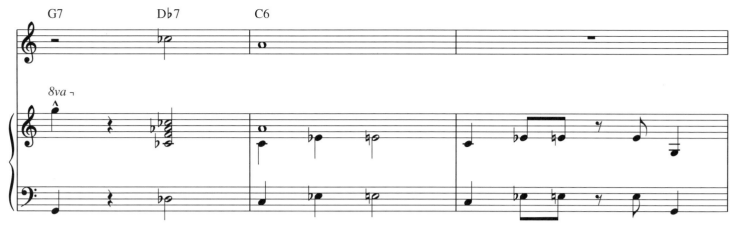

Mau - i. ___ And we'll feel the breeze and samp - le the

poi and go see Don Ho and I'll say, "Oh boy, how I love you,

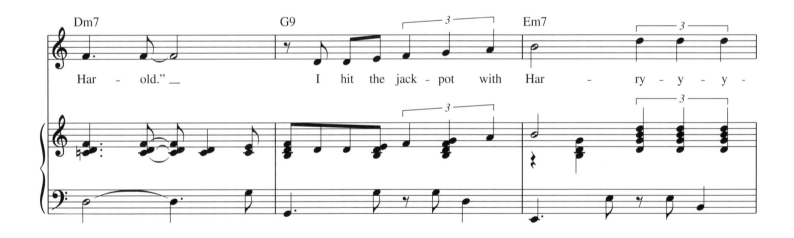

Har - old." ___ I hit the jack - pot with Har - ry - y - y -

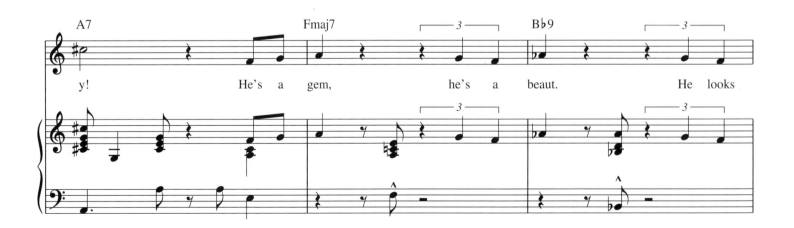

y! He's a gem, he's a beaut. He looks

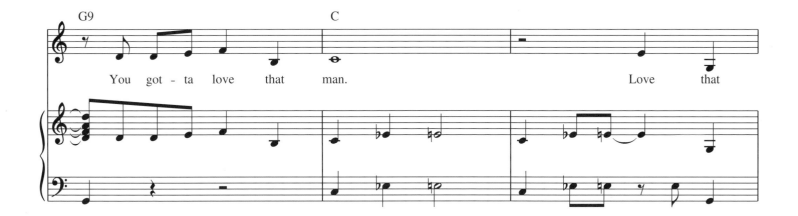

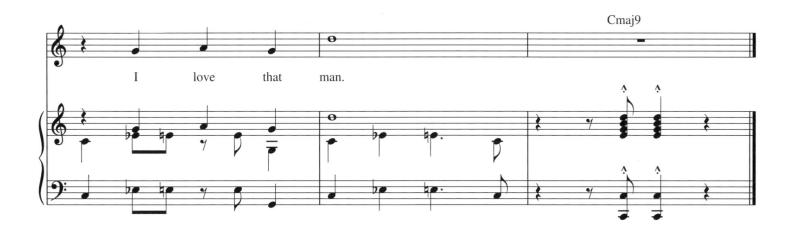

BIG-ASS ROCK

Words and Music by
DAVID YAZBEK

Rock Ballad

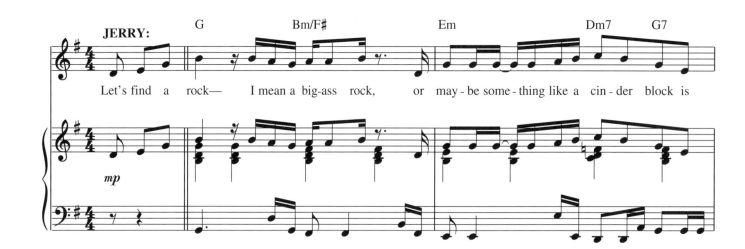

Let's find a rock— I mean a big-ass rock, or may-be some-thing like a cin-der block is

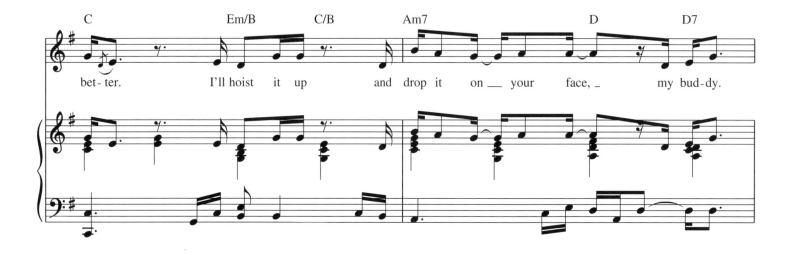

bet-ter. I'll hoist it up and drop it on __ your face, __ my bud-dy.

And just be-fore the lights go out you'll see my smile __ and you'll know you've got a friend. __

with a rock, who cares. _ I mean a big-ass rock. Or

rope. I got some qual-i-ty rope made for a man who's de-void o' hope _ like

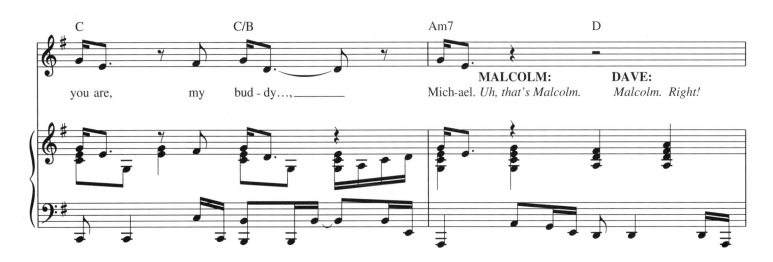

you are, my bud-dy…,_____

MALCOLM: *Mich-ael. Uh, that's Malcolm.* **DAVE:** *Malcolm. Right!*

DAVE: And I won't leave you _ swing-ing there, _ twitch-ing like a fish while you claw the air. _ I'll

34

grab your feet and, pal o' mine, I'll pull real hard and snap your spi - nal cord.

JERRY: This world is __ cold __ when you're a - lone __ and they ig - nore you. __

But don't kill your - self. __ **D & J:** We'll do it for __ you. You got a friend. __

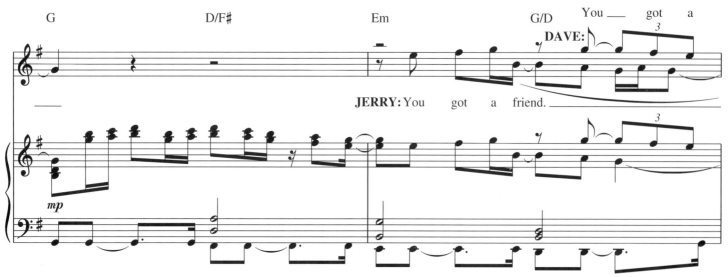

You __ got a
JERRY: You got a friend. _____
DAVE:

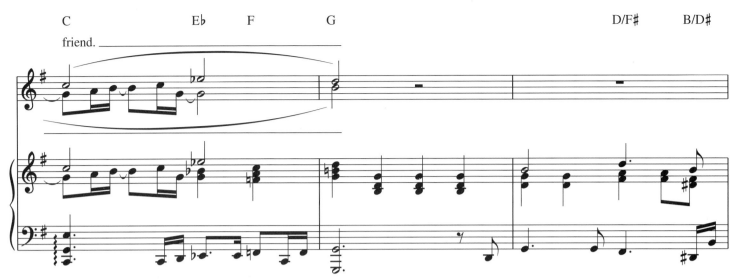

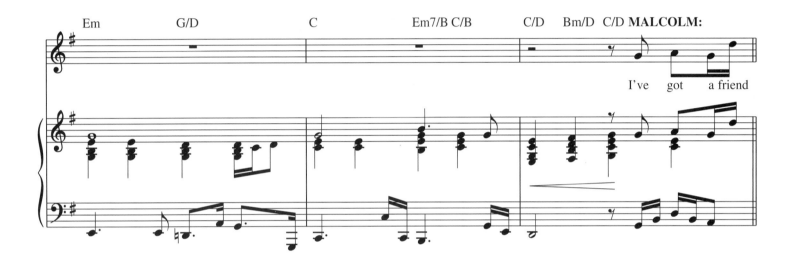

A *big*-ass rock!

buy you a beer __ with a Dra - no chas-er or dump you in the riv-er with a rock...

buy you a beer __ with a Dra - no chas-er or dump you in the riv-er with a rock...

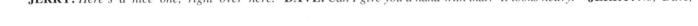

JERRY: *Here's a nice one, right over here.* **DAVE:** *Can I give you a hand with that? It looks heavy.* **JERRY:** *No, Dave,*

JERRY: It ain't heav-y, __ he's my friend. __ **DAVE:** *Come on, group hug.*

BIG BLACK MAN

Words and Music by
DAVID YAZBEK

Moderate Funk Rock

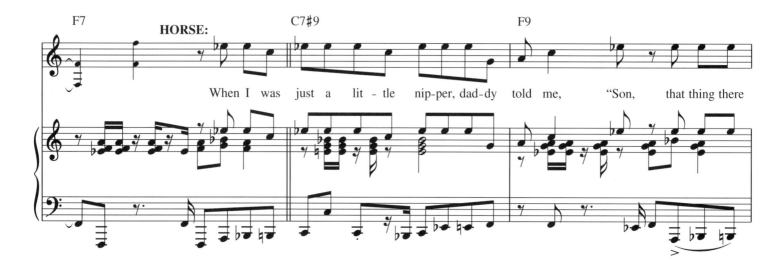

HORSE:

When I was just a lit-tle nip-per, dad-dy told me, "Son, that thing there

un-der-neath your zip-per can be lots of fun. When you get a lit-tle old-er, you'll

un-der - stand that ev-'ry wo-man in the world loves a big black man." Now I ain't

e - lite, I ain't no man of means but I got mean feet and my

dad-dy's genes. You just meet ___ me once and you'll ___ un-der - stand there ain't

noth-ing in the world like a big black man. 'Cause I'm big___ and I'm proud, sing-

-in' out loud. Danc - in' it since the day ___ I was born. Who's ___

___ got the tools? Who ___ breaks the rules? Get back and let a man do The

Pop - corn! I'm what your sis - ter and your ma-ma's al - ways think-ing of. They put my

pic - ture on the cov - er of the book of love. Nev - er need a line, ___ I don't

need no plan, _ 'cause there ain't noth-ing in the world like a— here I go, now hit me!

Hit me twice!

Hit me three times!

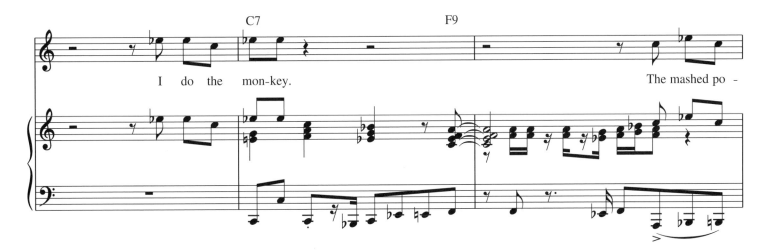

I do the mon-key. The mashed po -

ta - toes.   I do the jerk.

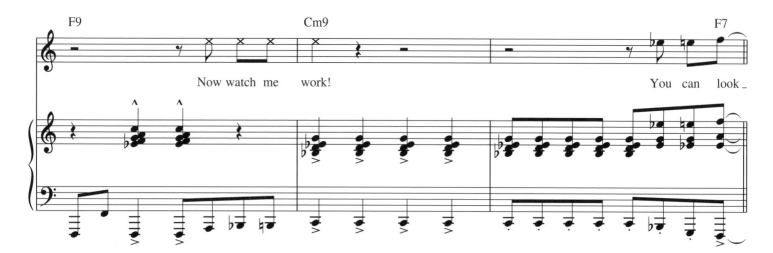

Now watch me   work!   You can look

up an' down,   All   o - ver town.   Ask   an - y - bod - y,   Ask

all a - round.   Who   knows the grooves?   Who   bust - a moves? I got the—

and the— and the— I'm what your sis-ter and your ma-ma's al-ways

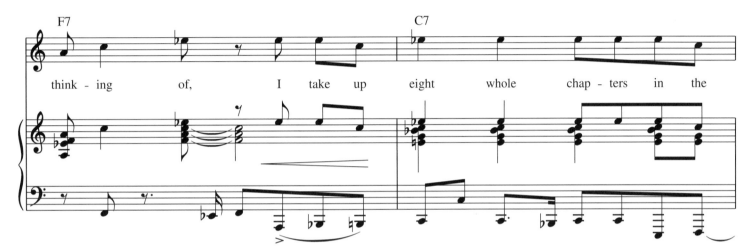

think-ing of, I take up eight whole chap-ters in the

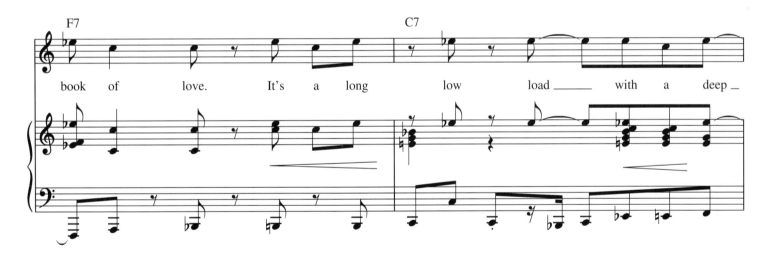

book of love. It's a long low load _____ with a deep _

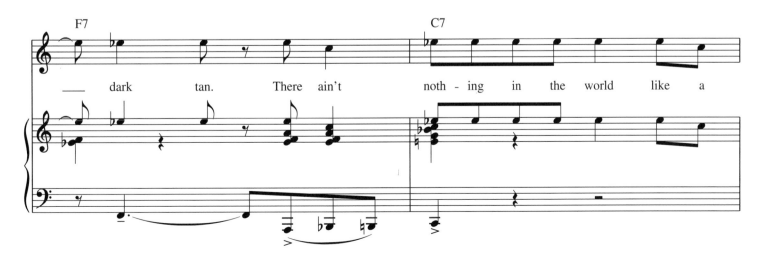

_ dark tan. There ain't noth-ing in the world like a

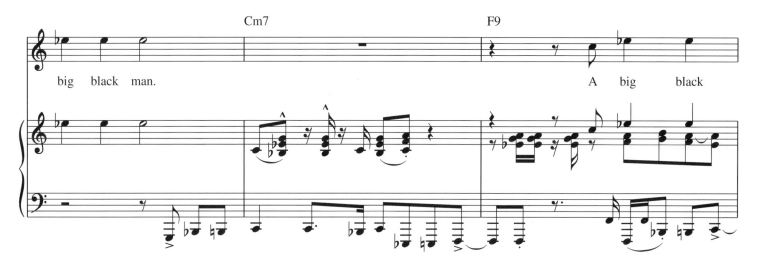

big black man.

Cm7   F9   A big black

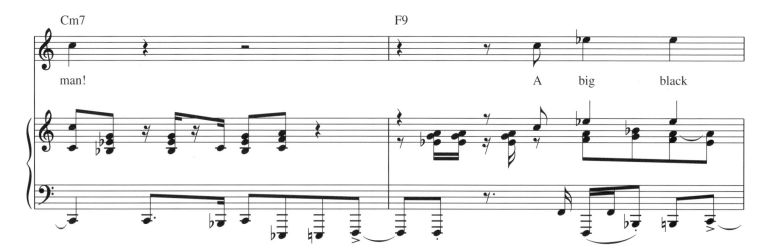

man!   A big black

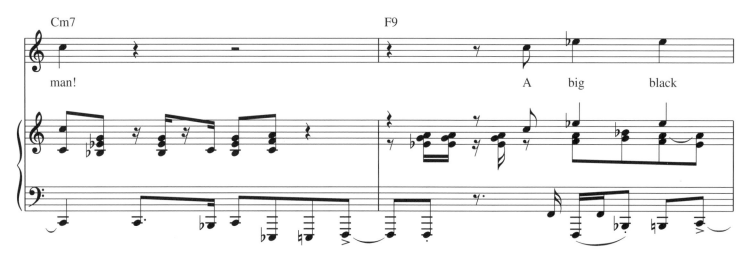

man!   A big black

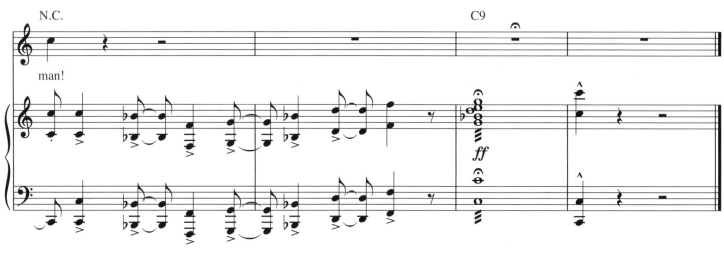

man!

YOU RULE MY WORLD

Words and Music by
DAVID YAZBEK

Slow ballad

DAVE:

Look at you. ____ You're ly - ing there. ____ I

feel your milk - y skin, ca - ress ____ your silk - y hair. ____ For

all these years ____ you've been with me, I tilt my chin and what ____ I see ____ is

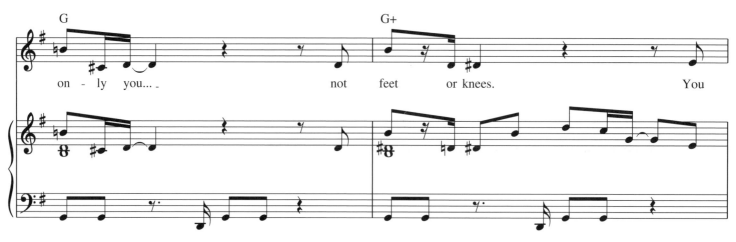

on - ly you.... not feet or knees. You

grum - ble and __ I stum - ble towards __ the Muen - ster cheese. __ I'm

in your spell, a chub-by fool __ and an - y - one __ can tell you rule my

world my world no mat-ter what I do __ you rule my

DAVE: world.

HAROLD: Look at you ____ my life, my dream _ my la - dy with the eight - y dol - lar

slum - ber cream, _ the hun - dred dol - lar hair - cuts, the nov -

- el - ty ____ ap - pli - an - ces _ we nev - er use, _ and all _

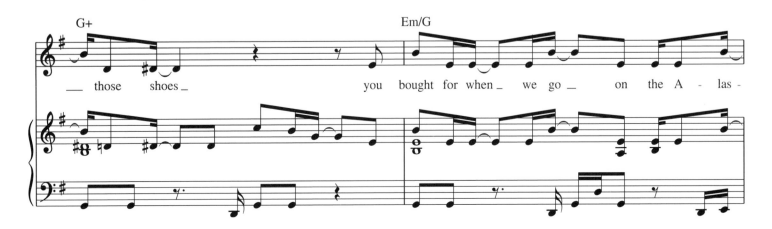

____ those shoes _ you bought for when _ we go _ on the A - las -

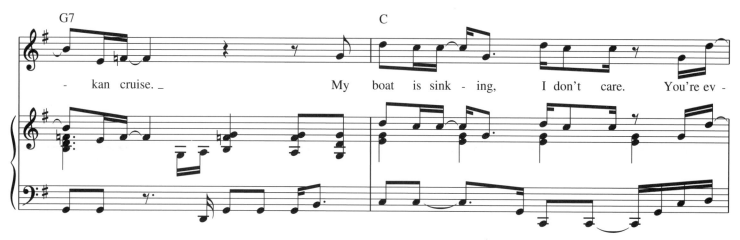

- kan cruise. _ My boat is sink - ing, I don't care. You're ev -

- 'ry - thing _ I want, you rule _ my world, my world, You're ev -

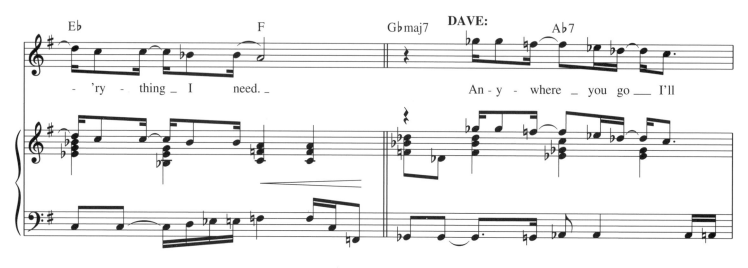

- 'ry - thing _ I need. _ An - y - where _ you go _ I'll

DAVE:

fol-low. An - y - thing _ you want _ I'll give _

HAROLD:
An - y - where I'll fol-low you. _____

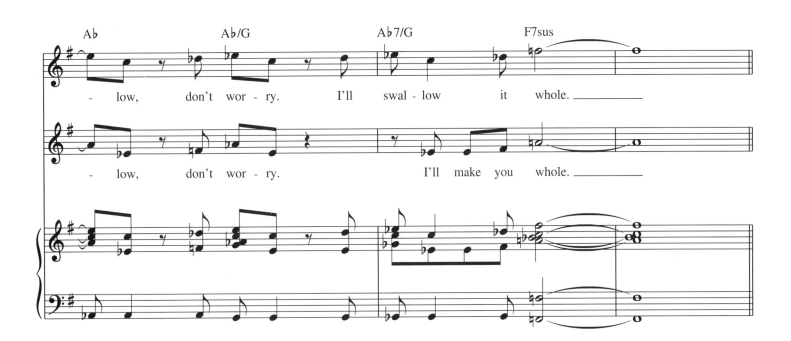

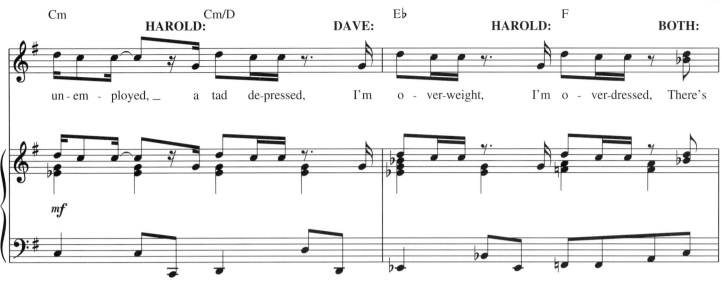

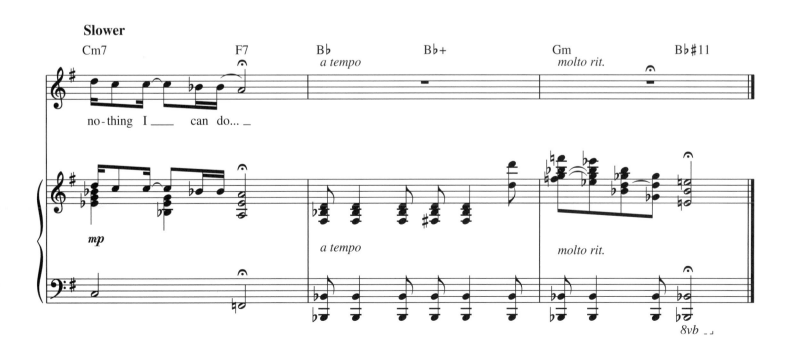

JEANETTE'S SHOWBIZ NUMBER

Words and Music by
DAVID YAZBEK

This gig's an ech-o of that time with Bud-dy Greck-o when we did the Des-ert Inn in fif-ty nine.

The danc-ing girls were clunk-y, the drum-mer was a junk-ie. But we

pulled the act to-geth-er and __ we killed 'em ev-'ry time. __ That hav-ing been said, frank-ly, I

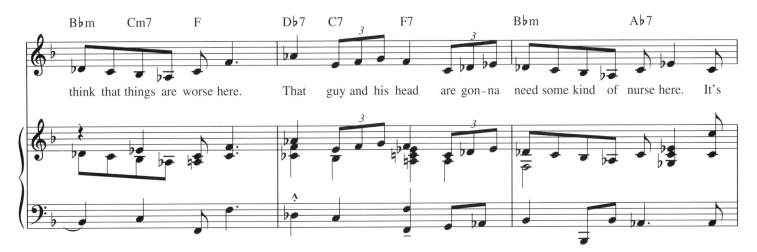

think that things are worse here. That guy and his head are gon-na need some kind of nurse here. It's

like a frig-gin' curse here. Things could be bet-ter— *So sue me, It's the truth—*

Things could be bet-ter 'round_ here. _ *It's an attitude problem. Seen it a million times.* I was

sub-bing with Stan Ken-ton in this seed-y club_ in Tren-ton when I heard my third di-vorce had just gone_

through. I could-a torn my heart out, but in-stead I got my chart out and I

gave 'em all a les-son in the way to play the blues. That hav-ing been said, some-thing is

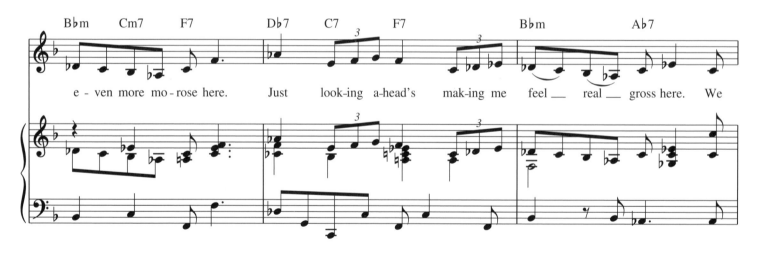

e - ven more mo-rose here. Just look-ing a-head's mak-ing me feel real gross here. We

are-n't e - ven close here. Things could be bet-ter. *Could they get any worse? I don't think so.*

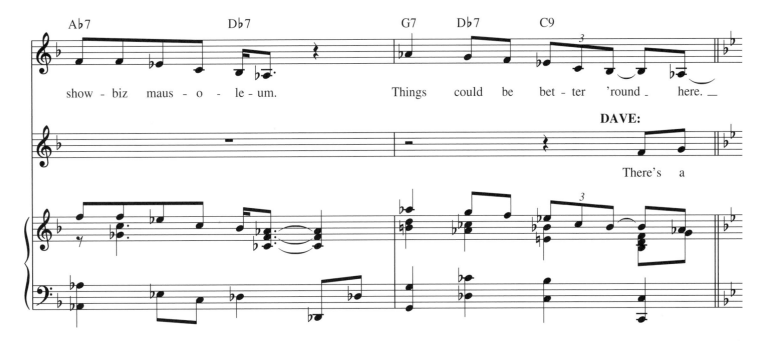

Throughout the song, the men's vocal lines sound an octave lower than written (standard practice);
Jeanette's vocal line is sung as written.

58

I could use some Ger - i - tol ___ de - liv - ered in ___ a hy - po. But I don't wan - na gripe— Oh

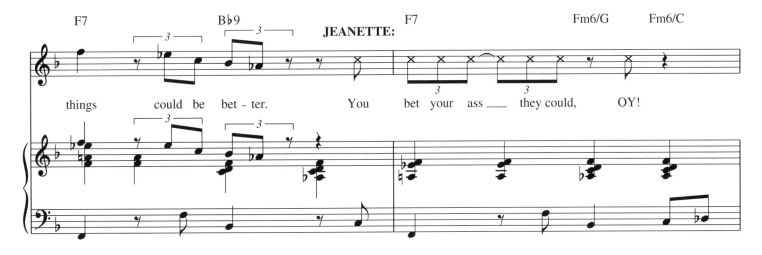

things could be bet - ter. You bet your ass ___ they could, OY!

Things could be bet - ter 'round ___ here. ___ I've

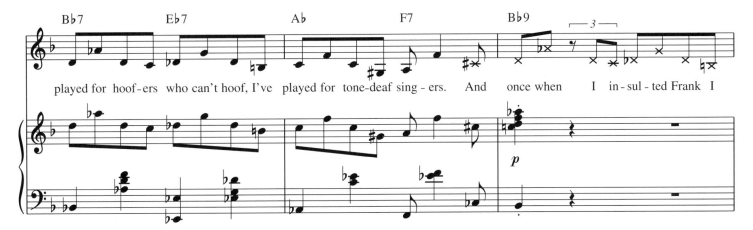

played for hoof - ers who can't hoof, I've played for tone-deaf sing - ers. And once when I in - sul - ted Frank I

played with bro-ken fing-ers. I've paid my dues. __ I know the blues— Of this, I can as-sure you. So

now I'll say it one last time __ 'cause I don't want to bore you. I

got some bad news for you.— Things _____

MEN:
Things could be bet-ter. They

BREEZE OFF THE RIVER

Words and Music by
DAVID YAZBEK

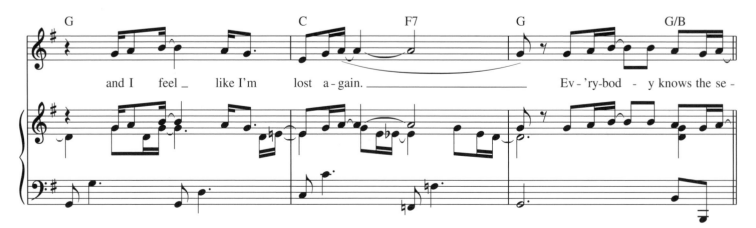

But when I look at you kid, it's like a mir - ror. It spins my

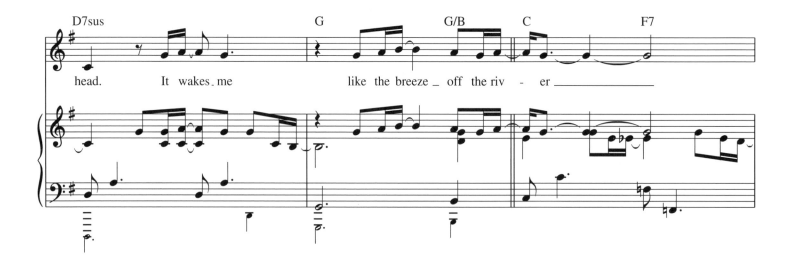

head. It wakes me like the breeze off the riv - er

ev - 'ry time I see your face. And it's strange but fa - mil -

- iar like a map of a bet - ter place.

And some - times I feel like I live in a shad-ow and

shad-ow's all ___ I see. ___ Then you jump straight up and you

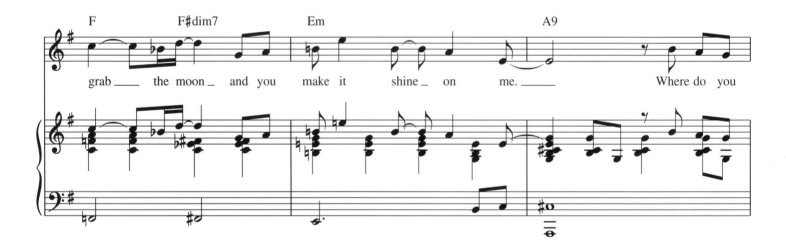

grab ___ the moon _ and you make it shine _ on me. ___ Where do you

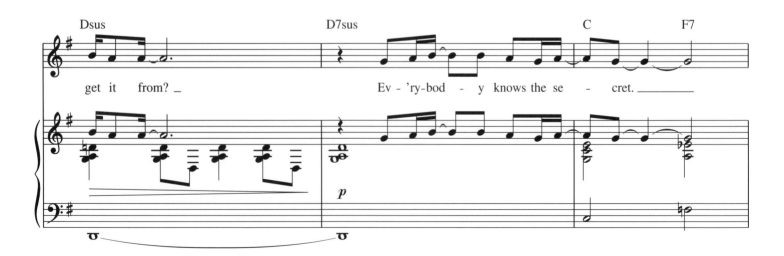

get it from? _ Ev - 'ry-bod - y knows the se - cret. ___

YOU RULE MY WORLD
(Reprise)

Words and Music by
DAVID YAZBEK

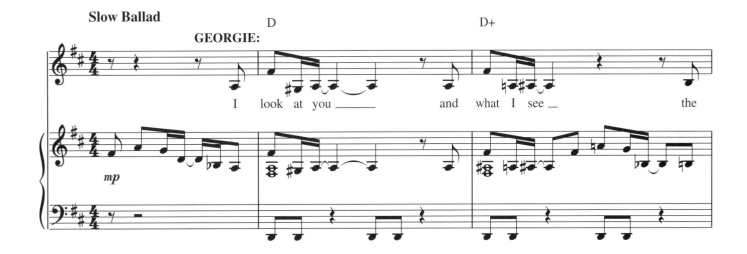

Slow Ballad

GEORGIE:

I look at you _____ and what I see _ the

on - ly man I ev - er loved _ in front of me. _ I chose _

_ you, Dave, _ it has - n't changed. You're ev - 'ry - thing _ I want. _ You rule my

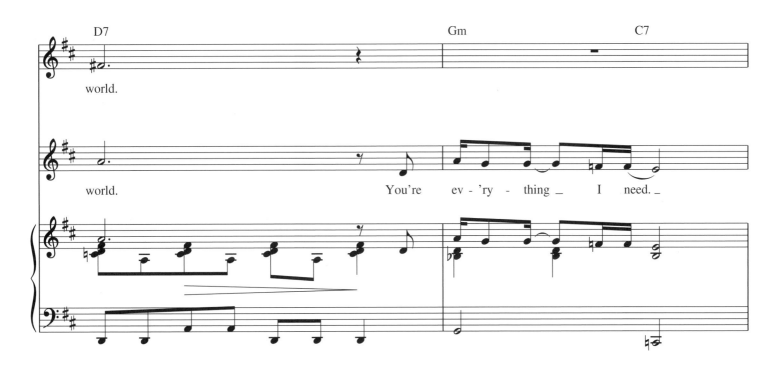

YOU WALK WITH ME

Words and Music by
DAVID YAZBEK

Moderately slow, but moving ahead

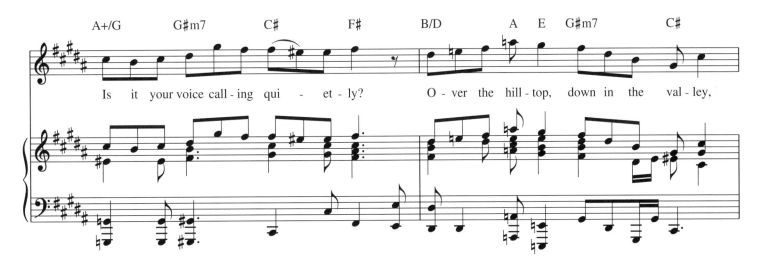

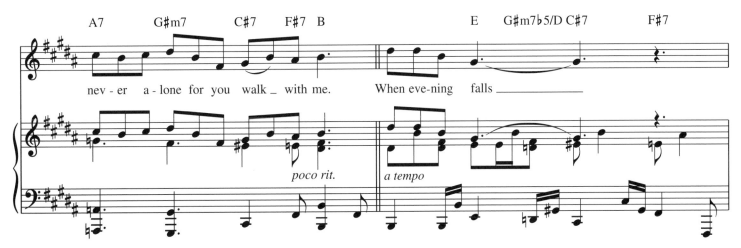

*Sing the top line melody in this section for a solo version of the song.

LET IT GO

Words and Music by
DAVID YAZBEK

_ se - ri-ous lit-tle sit - u - a - tion. Why don't we _ loos-en up and dance a - while?_

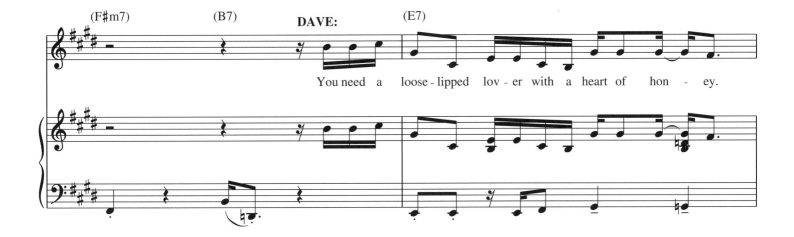

DAVE:

You need a loose - lipped lov - er with a heart of hon - ey.

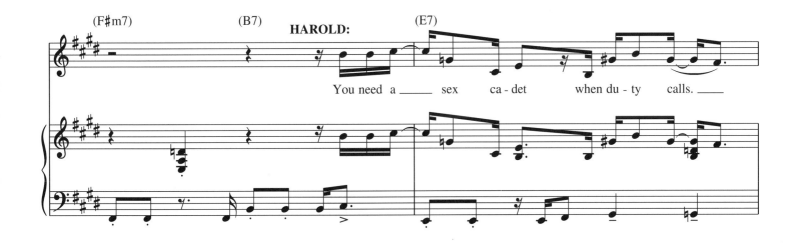

HAROLD:

You need a _____ sex ca - det when du - ty calls. _____

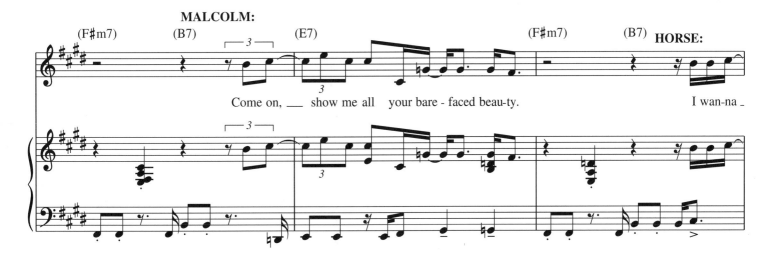

MALCOLM:

HORSE:

Come on, ___ show me all your bare - faced beau-ty. I wan-na _

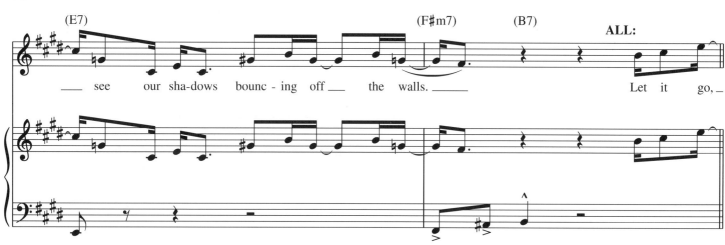

see our sha-dows bounc-ing off __ the walls. _____ Let it go, __

__ let it go. __ Loos-en up, yeah, let it go. __ Let it go, __

improvise a funky comp in the R.H.

__ let it go. __ It's al-right. ___ Let it go, __

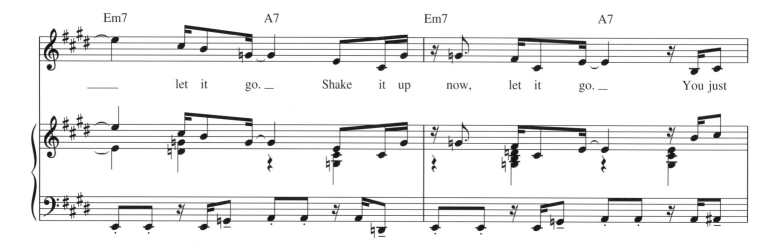

____ let it go. __ Shake it up now, let it go. __ You just

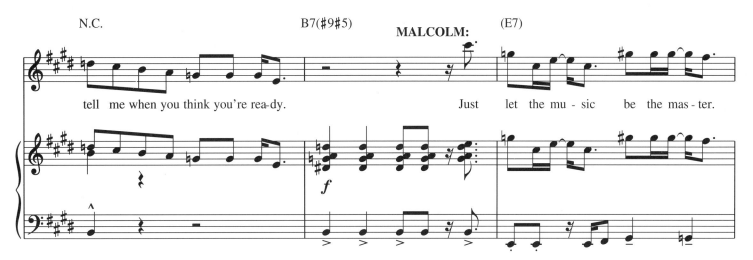

tell me when you think you're rea-dy. Just let the mu - sic be the mas - ter.

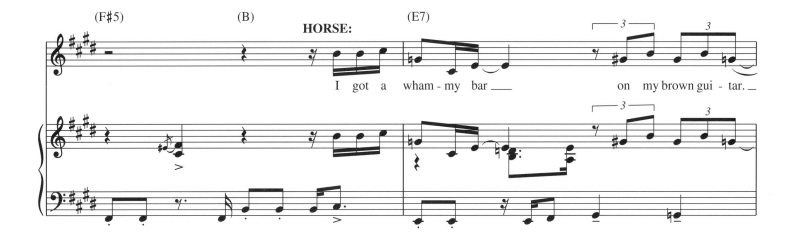

I got a wham - my bar ___ on my brown gui - tar. ___

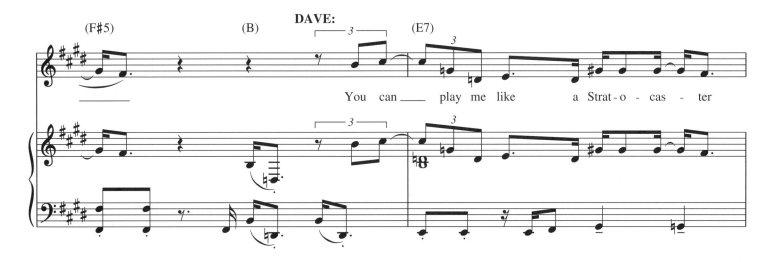

___ You can ___ play me like a Strat - o - cas - ter

Cause here I am __ and ba-by, there you are! __ Well I'm a ___

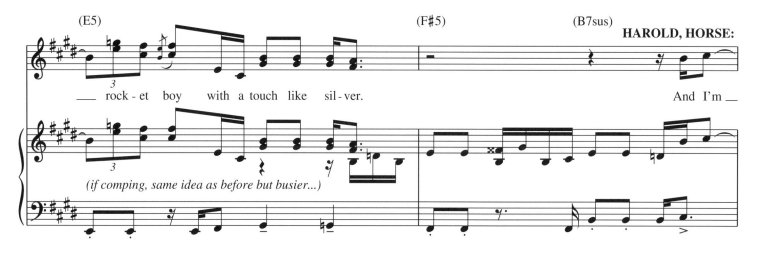

rock - et boy with a touch like sil - ver.

HAROLD, HORSE: And I'm ___

(if comping, same idea as before but busier...)

_crash - ing through your bed - room door. _____

E, J, M: And I'm

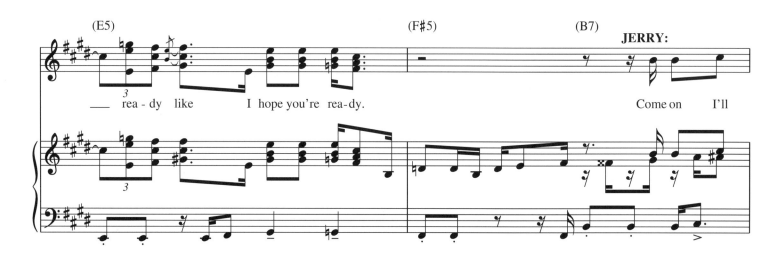

rea - dy like I hope you're rea - dy.

JERRY: Come on I'll

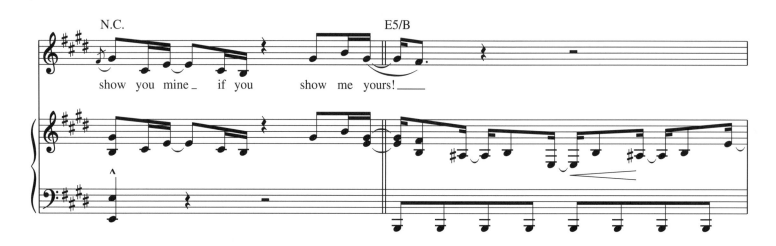

show you mine _ if you show me yours! _____

Let it go, _____ let it go. __ Loos - en up,

yeah, let it go. __ Let it go, ___ let it go. __ It's al - right. __

Let it go, ___ let it go. __ shake it up

now, let it go. ___ You just tell me when you think you're rea - dy.

Let it go, ___ let it go. ___ Loos - en up,

yeah, let it go. ___ Let it go, ___ let it go. ___ It's al - right. ___

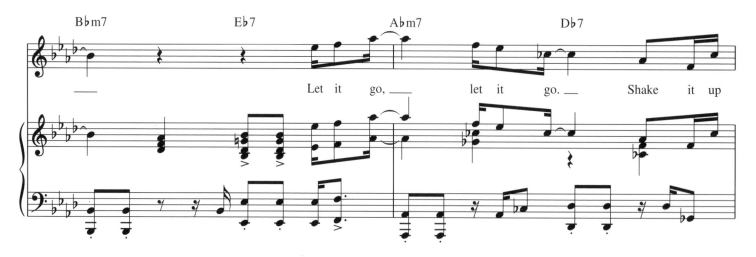

___ Let it go, ___ let it go. ___ Shake it up